To

From

Date

# Horse Tales from Heaven

TEXT BY **Rebecca E. Ondov**    ARTWORK BY **Chris Cummings**

HARVEST HOUSE PUBLISHERS

EUGENE, OREGON

# HORSE TALES FROM HEAVEN–GIFT EDITION

Text copyright © 2010 by Rebecca E. Ondov
Art copyright © Chris Cummings

Published by Harvest House Publishers
Eugene, Oregon 97402
www.harvesthousepublishers.com

ISBN 978-0-7369-2913-4

Blazing Ink, Inc. Artwork © by Chris Cummings, courtesy of Wild Wings, LLC,
2101 S. Highway 61, Lake City, MN 55041, www.wildwings.com.

*Design and production by Garborg Design Works, Savage, Minnesota*

Published in association with the Books & Such Literary Agency, 52 Mission Circle, Suite 122, PMB 170,
Santa Rosa, CA 95409-5370, www.booksandsuch.biz.

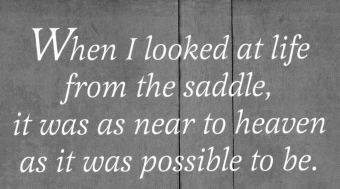

*When I looked at life from the saddle, it was as near to heaven as it was possible to be.*

FRANCES, COUNTESS OF WARWICK

# Contents

# Born Under Barbed Wire

I yawned and stretched as I slid open my second-story window. The whistle of a chickadee drifted through the still, cool air. Spring was unfolding her leaves and announcing the birth of another season in the Rocky Mountains. Dawn light danced over two mares nibbling new shoots of green grass, their colts nursing at their sides.

I squinted and frowned as I caught sight of Star, a sorrel mare, lying by the barbed-wire fence. Leaning on her front knees, she propped up her head. She looked exhausted. Behind her on the cold, hard ground lay a large gray blob. I pressed my nose against the window screen. *Oh my gosh! It's a foal! It's still in its placental sac...and it's under the barbed-wire fence.*

I ran down the stairs and hustled out the back door. The door slammed behind me. Star flinched, her eyes brimming with fear. I took a deep breath of crisp air. *Okay, Rebecca. Calm down so Star stays calm.* Casually I strolled through the dew-drenched grass toward the mare. Star nudged her foal's hind legs, issuing low and wondering nickers. The foal struggled, grunted, and propped itself on its front knees. Its head weaved and butted inside the sac. It looked like a child with a sheet over its head.

I slid through the fence just as the foal's sorrel head popped through. I crouched down and wiped its nostrils with my red bandana. Warm breath whispered across my hands. The foal's head wobbled as it tried to focus on me. Then it nickered. My heart leapt. *Wow, this creature thinks I'm its mom.* I slid back under the fence and grabbed the foal's hind legs through the sticky sac. I gently pulled it out of the membrane and under the fence, uphill and deeper into the pasture, Star following close behind us. I dropped its hind legs and moved to its head. The foal fastened its brown eyes on me and batted its long black eyelashes.

Star licked the baby clean while I paced around it taking inventory: a filly with four heavy-boned legs; black hooves; velveteen sorrel fur; a golden, wispy mane and tail; and fuzzy, teardrop-shaped ears. *Lord, what an awesome miracle!* Star nudged her newborn. The filly pulled her front legs under herself, pushed with her hind legs, grunted into a wheelbarrow shape, and pushed up. She plowed her nose into the ground and collapsed. The filly looked up, cocked her head side to side, and watched me. For the next 15 minutes she practiced standing...and crashing. Finally she stood, bracing her legs for stability. She looked at me and nickered, as if saying, "Look, Mom! I did it!"

My heart skipped a beat. *She's calling out to me.* Love for this little, sticky-wet, wobbly creature rose inside me. As I watched her toss her head, I had a strange thought: *Lord, does Your heart skip a beat when I call out to You? Do You think, "Why, it's Rebecca...and she's calling to Me!"*

Over the next few days the filly gradually lost interest in me as "mom," but I've never forgotten how my heart leapt at her first and second whinny. And in my mind's eye I see God's heart jump and His eyes twinkle when I talk with Him.

*We should behave like God's very own children, adopted into the bosom of his family, and calling him, "Father, Father."*

The Book of Romans 8:15 TLB

The mare set off for home with the speed of a swallow...and going as smoothly and silently. I never had dreamed of such a motion, fluent and graceful, and ambient, soft as the breeze flitting over the flowers, but swift as the summer lightning.

Richard Doddridge Blackmore

*Our sweetest experiences of affection are meant to be suggestions of that realm which is the home of the heart.*

Henry Ward Beecher

God took a handful of
southerly wind, blew
his breath upon
it, and created
the horse.

BEDOUIN LEGEND

I will not change my horse with any
that treads but on four pasterns.
When I bestride him I soar, I am
a hawk; he trots the air; the earth
sings when he touches it.

WILLIAM SHAKESPEARE

If God gives such
attention to the appearance
of wildflowers—most of
which are never even seen—
don't you think he'll attend
to you, take pride in you,
do his best for you?

THE BOOK OF MATTHEW

OUR BIRTH IS BUT A SLEEP AND A FORGETTING;
THE SOUL THAT RISES WITH US, OUR LIFE'S STAR,
HATH HAD ELSEWHERE ITS SETTING,
AND COMETH FROM AFAR;
NOT IN ENTIRE FORGETFULNESS,
AND NOT IN UTTER NAKEDNESS,
BUT TRAILING CLOUDS OF GLORY, DO WE COME
FROM GOD, WHO IS OUR HOME.

WILLIAM WORDSWORTH

# Snubbing Post

I shrugged on my jean jacket, pulled a halter off the hook, and slipped on my black cowboy hat. Wearing the hat felt silly. Even though I'd owned a horse and ridden since I was 14, I felt like a fraud. Every day when I chummed around *real* old-time cowboys I thought, *I wish I'd grown up on a ranch. If I'd grown up punching cows, then I would've earned the right to wear a cowboy hat.* My boss insisted the crew wear cowboy hats on pack trips, but until then... I took the hat off and hung it back on a peg. I opened the door and stepped out, closing it behind me.

Today I was going to catch the new chocolate-brown gelding. He'd been dubbed Dusty because he wasn't much to look at, just a middle-aged, snorty critter. I slipped the halter over my shoulder, attempting to hide it with my arm as I walked toward the pasture, but the horses spotted it and galloped to the other side. This was the hardest part of the job—trying to separate one of the wild-eyed creatures out of the herd in a ten-acre field. *If I'd grown up on a ranch, I would've learned to rope,* I groused.

I chased after the animals. I huffed and puffed as I zigzagged. Sweat rolled down my back. One-by-one I let the horses and mules spurt out until only Dusty stood in the corner. Snorting, his eyes brimmed with fear. I looked at the ground, lowered my voice, and spoke slowly, "Good boy. You must've had something pretty bad happen to you to make you this scared."

For the next half hour I'd take slow steps forward, talking, watching him squirm, then taking a step back as I let him get used to me. Finally, he let me rub his neck with the rope. I buckled on the halter. He followed me like he'd been handled. I heaved a sigh of relief as I led him out of the pasture. I tied him to the snubbing post—a four-foot-tall log firmly planted in the ground—and brushed him down.

Suddenly he jumped straight into the air. He came down snorting and blowing, the whites of his eyes showing.

I stepped back in shock. *Somebody must have really hurt this horse,* I thought again.

Dusty jumped forward and slammed into the snubbing post. It cracked. He hauled back again. Then he dug in with his hind legs, pulling backward. *Crack!* The snubbing post snapped, and the top of it whipped into Dusty's chest. He swung around, the broken post, held fast by the lead rope, slamming into his hindquarters. Dusty bolted down the driveway as if he were rounding the last turn at the Kentucky Derby.

I ran to the pickup, got in, and fired it up. I followed the cloud of dust. Three miles later the road wound between towering limestone cliffs. I rounded the bend. There was Dusty. White lather blanketed him from head to hoof. He stood calmly, munching grass in a ditch.

*My beautiful! My beautiful!*
*That standest meekly by*
*With thy proudly arch'd and glossy neck,*
*And dark and fiery eye;*
*The stranger hath thy bridle-rein—*
*Thy master hath his gold.*
*Fleet-limb'd and beautiful, farewell!*
*Thou art sold, my steed—thou art sold!*

LADY CAROLINE SHERIDAN NORTON

Every day we live is a priceless gift of God, loaded with possibilities to learn something new, to gain fresh insights into His great truths.

DALE EVANS ROGERS

*The wildest colts only make the best horses.*

PLUTARCH

Next to him was the snubbing post, still securely tied to the rope.

He'd spooked because of the abuse in his past. The harder he ran from it, the harder the post beat him. When he quit running, he discovered that the post quit beating him. So instead of running from it, now he used it as a starting place. From that point on, Dusty was transformed into the calmest, most levelheaded horse for guests on the place.

The next morning I took Dusty's lesson to heart. I quit tying my past to a snubbing post and used it as a starting place. I slipped on my cowboy hat and headed to the corral. I hadn't been raised on a ranch, but I earned my hat each day as I slogged through the mud chasing critters and peppered my old-time cowboy friends with questions every night, learning as much as possible about this new lifestyle. They gave me the leg up I needed to ride confidently into the wilderness.

*It is not enough for a man to learn how to ride; he must learn how to fall.*

MEXICAN PROVERB

THE GOD WHO GAVE US LIFE, GAVE US LIBERTY AT THE SAME TIME.

THOMAS JEFFERSON

*I can't tell you how much I long for you to enter this wide-open, spacious life...Open up your lives. Live openly and expansively!*

THE BOOK OF SECOND CORINTHIANS

# The Seeing Eye

Under the pines in the Danaher Valley, dozens of horses and mules stood tied to the rope corral while the wranglers removed their saddles. The August afternoon heat and the smell of horse sweat lured a drone of horse flies. The stock swished their tails and stomped their feet, trying to shake off the hungry flies. A tall, raw-boned, cinnamon-colored appaloosa with no mane and a rattail stood tied at the end of the row. Her ribs showed from hundreds of rugged miles on pack trips.

I took off my black cowboy hat and ran my fingers through my blond hair. *What am I going to do about Melinda?* The last five days of grueling mountain trails combined with four nights on a picket rope had sheered weight off her. I had to keep her on the picket rope because she was night-blind. *But she needs more feed than she can get staked out on a picket.* We didn't have any grain left, we were miles from supplies, and there were five more days left on this trip. *What can I do?*

On summer trips, at night we turned the horses and mules loose to graze, letting the folds of the mountains and the thick forest serve as a natural corral. *She needs to be turned out with the herd to graze all night.*

I hollered to a wrangler, "Brian, turn Melinda loose tonight."

"But she's..."

"She needs the feed. If you turn the herd out now, instead of after dinner, we can keep an eye on her." I slipped on my hat and walked to the kitchen area where the guests were filling their plates with tossed salad and spaghetti. Instead of joining them, I carried my plate and my steaming coffee out in the meadow. Sitting against a tree, I watched Melinda and mentally beat myself up. *What was I thinking, turning her loose?* I stabbed the noodles with my fork.

*After dark, if the herd moves faster than a walk, how will she be able to keep up? What if she panics and takes off—running blind?* As the sun sank, the shadows exaggerated Melinda's ribs. I weakly surrendered, *God, You know Melinda needs the feed. Please watch over her tonight.* But I was haunted. *Should I bother such a busy God by asking Him to watch over a horse?*

Melinda walked over to Roman, a sorrel mule with a white mane that was cut short—"roached" they called it. Puzzled, I thought, *That's odd. Why is Melinda doing that? Horses generally don't care for mules.*

When twilight settled over the valley and the moon rose, Roman picked up his head and chortled at Melinda. Melinda positioned herself behind the mule. Then she did an incredibly strange thing: She rested her head on Roman's rump. Like a truck hitched to a gooseneck trailer, they lumbered through the moonlit meadow. When Roman smelled a delicious spot, he stopped and cropped grass. Melinda did too. When Roman was ready to move, he lifted his head and chortled for Melinda. Once again she rested her head on his rump, and they wandered off.

*How amazing! He's acting as her seeing-eye dog. Only You, God, could make this happen.* God *did* care about that raw-boned, rattailed horse in the boonies. And He cares about my concerns too. He's just waiting for me to ask. Grabbing my plate, I strolled toward the guests huddled around the crackling campfire. I knew Melinda was safe.

*Don't worry about anything, but pray about everything. With thankful hearts offer up your prayers and requests to God.*

THE BOOK OF PHILIPPIANS CEV

We ought to do good to others as simply and naturally as a horse runs, or a bee makes honey, or a vine bears grapes season after season without thinking of the grapes it has borne.

MARCUS AURELIUS

THE WIND OF HEAVEN IS THAT WHICH BLOWS BETWEEN A HORSE'S EARS.

ARABIAN PROVERB

*There is something about the outside of a horse that is good for the inside of a man.*

WINSTON CHURCHILL

*A horse! a horse! my kingdom for a horse!*

WILLIAM SHAKESPEARE

# Buck 'n' Run

The autumn sunshine filtered through my office window, casting shadows across my checklist of horses to be used for tomorrow's trip. With my pencil, I drew a line through all those who were injured. Then I drew a big fat "X" through "Amarillo." He was new and had a horrible habit of bucking.

I assigned the available horses to guests and crew, but in the end, I was one short. *God, should I buy those horses I looked at last week?* I doodled as I considered my options. *I don't know if there'll be enough pasture if I do.* I glanced at my watch: 9:30. *I better get rolling.* Erasing the "X," I wrote my name next to Amarillo.

The next morning, a cloud of dust billowed behind the gold pickup as I pulled into the trailhead parking lot.

When I got to the corral and caught Amarillo, I lectured him. "You'd better behave today." Amarillo rolled his eyes from side to side as I tossed the saddle onto his back. Gathering the reins, I stepped into the saddle and kicked him into a trot. Amarillo's hooves drummed on the hard-packed dirt trail. After a while I relaxed, watching the forest come to life around me.

Suddenly Amarillo exploded, jumping straight up. Mid-air, he bowed his neck and arched his back. His hooves hit the ground with stiff legs, and he dropped his right shoulder.

I sailed through the air...and landed head-first in the dirt.

As suddenly as he'd started to buck, Amarillo quit. He glanced at me lying on the trail and then dropped his nose into a patch of green grass.

Moaning, I sat up. I ran my hand through my hair and winced. A large knot was growing above my right eye. Slowly, I managed to stand. Scooping up my hat, I walked toward Amarillo.

Acting as if he didn't notice me, he casually stepped away.

"I know what you're doing," I said.

Amarillo bobbed his head, as if to say, "Catch me if you can." Then he trotted away, over the next hill. I shouted after him, "You'd better not do this to me all the way to camp!" It was 11 miles away.

I wasn't worried about losing him because he knew where camp was. But I had a horse to ride—*not to walk behind*. I boiled as I hiked the trail, trying to catch a glimpse of him. Topping a hill, I saw a long-brown ribbon on the trail. He'd stepped on and broken a brand-new rein. *That rascal!* Rounding the bend, I groaned when I saw Yellowjacket Creek gurgling over some rocks. I jumped over as far as I could, and then scampered to the bank, my leather boots sloshing with each step.

I jogged through the tall pines and bushwhacked through snowberry brush. I clawed my way up a steep slope. When Amarillo spotted me, he trotted around the bend and out of sight. The next time I saw him was eight miles later, when my boots squished down the trail into

To learn all that a horse could teach, was a world of knowledge, but only a beginning... Look into a horse's eye and you instantly know if you can trust him.

Mary O'Hara

Be still, and know that I am God!

The Book of Psalms nlt

the camp. He stood in the hay shed, eating grain out of a barrel he'd pushed the lid back on. Lifting his head up, grain and slobber dripping from his mouth, he eyed me with a "What took you so long?" attitude.

I grabbed the remaining rein and pulled his head next to mine. "What do you think you're doing—making *me* walk all the way into camp? You only stopped when *you* got what *you* wanted—the grain!"

Then deep within my spirit I heard, "He's acting just like you."

*Me?* It was true. Yesterday when I'd asked God about buying the horses, I'd barely paused for a breath before moving on to the next thing on *my* agenda. I hadn't waited for God to answer.

I thought about all the times I'd bucked and run from God. For the next hour, I forced myself to be quiet and trained my thoughts on God. He spoke to me through the Holy Spirit. I wasn't to buy any more horses until spring. By the time I lit the woodstove to start dinner, I knew I'd just learned a priceless lesson—to wait on God.

*Endurance is the crowning quality,*
*And patience all the passion of great hearts.*

James Russell Lowell

We have only to be patient, to pray, and to do His will, according to our present light and strength, and the growth of the soul will go on.

### WILLIAM ELLERY CHANNING

Under his spurning feet, the road
Like an arrowy Alpine river flowed,
And the landscape sped away behind
Like an ocean flying before the wind.

### THOMAS BUCHANAN READ, "SHERIDAN'S RIDE"

*Each morning you listen to my prayer, as I bring my requests to you and wait for your reply.*

THE BOOK OF PSALMS CEV

# Bobbing for Apples

I stood peering out the window that overlooked my horse pasture and ogled my new majestic Tennessee Walker mare. Only hours ago I'd unloaded her from the horse trailer. I still couldn't believe she was mine!

Her black coat glimmered blue in the sunlight, and her long, black tail flowed to the ground. She looked magnificent, like she belonged in a king's stable. With an arched neck and a composed, stately manner she explored her new domain and sniffed around the barn. Then she strolled over to the watering tank and nuzzled the sides. She lightly chewed on the top edge. Making a scooping motion with her head, she splashed water over the side. She smelled the water on the ground and pawed the newly created mud. Stepping next to the tank, she dunked her head—all the way up to her eyes.

I pushed my nose against the window. She pulled her head out and shook the water off her nose, and then plunged her head underwater—way past her ears! I'd never seen a horse do anything like that. *Is something wrong?*

I flew out the door. My boots pounded down the dirt trail, and I squeezed through the fence. My new mare ambled over to greet me, water dripping off her chin. I scratched her soggy forehead. "Are you feeling okay?" I asked. My mind whirled. *Could she have a fever?* I felt her throat. She wasn't sweaty or clammy. Puzzled, I perched on the edge of the water tank and watched her for a few minutes. She seemed normal—until I turned to go. She lumbered

> Go anywhere in England where there are natural, wholesome, contented, and really nice English people; and what do you always find? That the stables are the real centre of the household.
>
> GEORGE BERNARD SHAW

*Laughter is not at all a bad beginning for a friendship.*

OSCAR WILDE

to the water tank, pawed with her front foot, and then submerged her whole head—this time she must have gone all the way to the bottom of the tank. It looked like she was bobbing for apples. *There's something really wrong. Horses don't do this! Is she sick? Crazy?*

I ran up to the house and called Connie, the previous owner. "I think there's something wrong. The mare's acting really strange." I went on, explaining the problem.

Connie giggled. "Rebecca, there's nothing to worry about. She's dunking her head all the way to the bottom so she can pull out the drain plug. She wants the water to run over the ground so she can play in the puddle."

Relieved, I laughed out loud. "I guess I bought a horse with a sense of humor."

24

*A good laugh
is sunshine in
a house.*

WILLIAM THACKERAY

$T$ake all the pleasures of all the spheres,
And multiply each through endless years,
One minute of Heaven is worth them all.

THOMAS MOORE

*The grand
essentials to
happiness in this
life are something
to do, something to
love, and something
to hope for.*

JOSEPH ADDISON

$A$ cheerful look
brings joy to the heart;
good news makes for
good health.

THE BOOK OF PROVERBS NLT

I CAST LOOSE MY BUFF-COAT, EACH HOLSTER LET FALL,

SHOOK OFF BOTH MY JACK-BOOTS, LET GO BELT AND ALL,

STOOD UP IN THE STIRRUPS, LEANED, PATTED HIS EAR,

CALLED MY ROLAND HIS PET-NAME, MY HORSE WITHOUT PEER—

CLAPPED MY HANDS, LAUGHED AND SUNG, ANY NOISE, BAD OR GOOD,

TILL AT LENGTH INTO AIX, ROLAND GALLOPED AND STOOD.

ROBERT BROWNING, *HOW THEY BROUGHT THE NEWS FROM GHENT*

# Greener Pastures

My car's headlights pierced the night, and the tires squeaked through the snow as I turned into my driveway. Groaning, I stared at the snow banks that lined both sides of the drive and were taller than my car. It was one o'clock in the morning. I'd just flown in from Texas where I'd visited my good friend Sandy, who was attending Bible school. The Texas sun had warmed my bones, and the God-centered atmosphere had thawed my heart. I longed for that kind of setting.

Pulling up to the metal gate, I hopped out and glanced across the pasture. Other than a couple narrow paths the horses had created, the pasture was covered with a smooth, four-foot-deep blanket of snow that glowed in the moonlight. I pushed open the gate. The headlights illuminated the horses on the other side of the electric fence, tromping through the snow to greet me. Dazzle, a black mare, tossed her head. Czar, my bay gelding, nickered, and my brown mule named Little Girl brayed. I shouted, "Hi, guys! You won't believe what I brought home for you!" When Sandy and I had walked through knee-high grass in Texas, I'd gotten this crazy idea: *Why not bring home a small trash bag of fresh grass for the horses?* So I did.

Popping the hatch of my red station wagon, I pulled out the bag. Grabbing a wad of grass, I marched through the snow to the fence. When the critters smelled the "green," all three of their noses came up. They sniffed the air in disbelief as they rushed to me. I doled a handful to Little Girl. She grabbed it and trotted away as Czar tossed his head, pinned back his ears, and told her to scoot. I reached in the bag with both hands and held them out to Czar and Dazzle. "You're only getting one handful tonight. I don't want you to get sick because it's so rich." They savored it. I yawned, "There will be more in the morning," I commented as I turned to go.

I jumped into the car, pulled down the driveway, and parked in the garage. Too tired to carry the suitcase into the house, I went straight to bed. I fell asleep holding on to nice memories of the faith-centered atmosphere of Sandy's school. When the morning sun streamed into my bedroom, I stretched lazily and walked over to my window. The sun glinted off the snow. But instead of a smooth blanket, the snow was in humps and bumps all over the

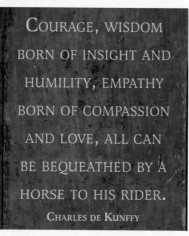

COURAGE, WISDOM BORN OF INSIGHT AND HUMILITY, EMPATHY BORN OF COMPASSION AND LOVE, ALL CAN BE BEQUEATHED BY A HORSE TO HIS RIDER.
CHARLES DE KUNFFY

pasture. I looked again, squinting. The whole pasture looked as if it had been dug up with a backhoe. I frowned as I cast a glance from one end to the other. *What had happened last night?*

Then I saw my three critters, huddled in the fence corner and digging in the snow like they were searching for hidden treasure. As they pawed, the snow flew in heaps behind them. I realized they were looking for more green grass! Clearly, they'd spent the whole night digging. There wasn't hardly a spot they'd missed. As I laughed, I heard from deep within my spirit, "If you will dig into My Word like they have the pasture, you'll create a God-centered atmosphere in your heart."

I pressed my nose against the window, watching Czar push his muzzle along the ground, trying to smell something green. *Lord, I am hungry for You, just like they're hungry for fresh grass.* I walked into the kitchen and turned on the coffee. Snuggling into my rocker, I opened my Bible and settled in for a good, long read.

*Reflect upon your present blessings, of which every man has many.*

CHARLES DICKENS

Wherever man has left his footprint in the long ascent from barbarism to civilization, we will find the hoofprint of a horse beside it.

JOHN TROTWOOD MOORE

WE THROW OPEN OUR DOORS
TO GOD AND DISCOVER AT
THE SAME MOMENT THAT HE
HAS ALREADY THROWN OPEN
HIS DOOR TO US. WE FIND
OURSELVES STANDING WHERE
WE ALWAYS HOPED WE MIGHT
STAND—OUT IN THE WIDE OPEN
SPACES OF GOD'S GRACE AND
GLORY, STANDING TALL AND
SHOUTING OUR PRAISE.

THE BOOK OF ROMANS

*There is not one blade of grass,
there is no color in this world that
is not intended to make us rejoice.*

JOHN CALVIN

*The basest horn of [my horse's] hoof is
more musical than the pipe of Hermes.*

WILLIAM SHAKESPEARE, *HENRY V*

# Angels in the Snow

Sunlight streamed into the tent. I squinted at my alarm clock... *8:30*. I'd only been asleep a few hours because I had split shifts as the hunting camp cook. I groaned and rolled on my side. The steam from my breath floated in the air. It had snowed a few inches last night, and the brilliant sunlight glistened off the snow, making it look like I had floodlights inside the tent. I sighed. *Might as well get up...another day of endless work...just like yesterday.*

Like a zombie, I dressed and trudged through the snow to the cook tent. The black, enamelware coffeepot simmered on the woodstove. Grabbing my blue mug, I poured. The coffee was thick enough to float a horseshoe. I sat at the plank table and stared at the spiral notebook. Every day my "chore list" was seemingly endless: chop kindling, fuel lanterns, sweep guest tents, make a fresh loaf of bread, bake pecan pies, and brush Czar.

Robotically, I trudged through the snow to the corral to collect the lanterns from the tack shed and to brush my horse. The wooden corral gate creaked as I slipped through. Czar lay basking in the warm sun that glinted off his bay coat. Fresh, fluffy snow lay around him. Only his ears twitched and his eyes rolled as he watched me. I laughed, "Time to get up, sleepyhead."

Czar stretched his legs, sweeping the snow aside, and then curled them toward his belly. He reminded me of when I was a child. I'd lay flat on my back in the snow and sweep my arms and legs in a jumping-jack motion to make a snow angel in the powder.

Czar lazily rolled onto his back and wiggled. Then he flopped onto his side. He curled his legs underneath him, heaved to his feet, and shook off clumps of snow.

With delight I admired the horse angel. When Czar flopped on his side, the imprint from his front leg smacking the ground almost looked like a trumpet. The horse angel was blowing it. Momentarily I forgot my routine. The snow around me glittered in the sunlight like a sea of diamonds. Each flake shimmered rays of light: blues, greens, golds, and reds. I glanced around the pasture where horses had laid in the snow. Angels were everywhere, and they were all blowing trumpets. I could almost hear the regal notes.

I'd been so absorbed in my "get it done" routine that I'd almost missed it. Heaps of snowflakes stood on the wooden fence rails. A squirrel sat above me, scolding me loudly. His tail switched, knocking piles of snow from the pine needles and onto my head. I laughed and brushed it out of my hair. I inhaled a deep breath of crisp air. All around me, the blue sky outlined glistening, snowy peaks. *How many times have I walked in and out of the cook tent doing chores without noticing any of this?* I wondered.

For the rest of the day, I gawked at God's creation. With a happy heart, my chores didn't seem like drudgery. The day flew past. I even found myself humming while I washed dishes that night.

## Blessings star forth forever;

For the wonderful brain of man
However mighty its force
Had never achieved its lordly plan
Without the aid of a horse.

ELLA WILCOX

*When much in the woods as a little girl, I was told that the snake would bite me, that I might pick a poisonous flower or Goblins kidnap me; but I went along and met no one but angels.*

EMILY DICKINSON

*Teach us delight in simple things, and mirth that has no bitter springs.*

RUDYARD KIPLING

YOU HAVE SHOWN ME THE PATH OF LIFE, AND YOU MAKE ME GLAD BY BEING NEAR TO ME. SITTING AT YOUR RIGHT SIDE, I WILL ALWAYS BE JOYFUL.

THE BOOK OF PSALMS CEV

In God's wildness lies the hope of the world—the great fresh unblighted, unredeemed wilderness. The galling harness of civilization drops off, and wounds heal ere we are aware.

JOHN MUIR

*but a curse is like a cloud, it passes.*

PHILIP JAMES BAILEY

# Blind Colt

It was my favorite time of year—May. The snow had melted out of the valley, the robins had returned, and yesterday my mare, Snipe, had given birth to a most precious colt. I named him Obadiah.

The weathered barn door groaned as I slipped into the stall and dropped hay into the feeder. Snipe stuffed her mouth hungrily while I ruffled Obadiah's red-velveteen coat. He cocked his head to the side. His long, black eyelashes rimmed beautiful brown eyes.

I told Snipe, "What a beautiful, healthy boy you have."

Obadiah turned as if listening to me. Then he switched his tail and whirled around. I watched in horror as he ran headlong into the wall, recovered, and then bounded and charged into the wall again. He crumpled to the ground, and then gathered his legs and lurched to his feet.

Snipe tenderly brushed her muzzle across the top of his back and down his legs, checking him over. *Snipe is treating him like he's fragile,* I noted.

*Could he be blind?* I snuggled him next to my body. I slowly waved my hand in front of his face. His eyes didn't follow. I moved my finger toward him until I nearly touched his eyeball. He didn't blink.

I could never turn a blind horse out with the herd. He'd always be at risk. He could run into the barbed-wire fence, off a cliff, or lead other horses astray. My heart was shattered. I knew I'd never find a home for him. *I'll have to put him down before I get too attached.*

I went about the rest of the day in a daze, my thoughts on the colt. That night the colt drifted in and out of my dreams.

The next day I rubbed my eyes as I leaned against the exam room counter at the vet clinic.

*My horse's feet are as swift as rolling thunder*
*He carries me away from all my fears*
*And when the world threatens to fall asunder*
*His mane is there to wipe away my tears.*

BONNIE LEWIS

Dr. Roulette held the stethoscope to Obadiah's ribs and then checked his eyes. "You're right. I'm afraid he's blind."

My tears blurred the room. I rubbed my forehead and looked at my boots.

"If you want, I'll put him down." Dr. Roulette caressed the colt's soft fur. Obadiah nibbled on his blue shirt. Dr. Roulette softly said, "This might be a long shot, but I heard about a veterinary school that has done research on blindness in colts. I'll give them a call, maybe there's something we can do." He rubbed Obadiah's neck. "You don't have anything to lose by waiting a couple days."

Dr. Roulette's words sparked a glimmer of hope in my heart. I nodded. *I have to give it a try.*

I drove the stock truck home and led Snipe and Obadiah into the stall. Then I waited

> *I heard a neigh. Oh, such a brisk and melodious neigh as that was! My very heart leaped with delight at the sound.*
>
> NATHANIEL HAWTHORNE

> The LORD God gives me the right words to encourage the weary.
>
> THE BOOK OF ISAIAH CEV

anxiously by the phone. On the second day, Dr. Roulette called with a question, "Do you know the exact date Snipe was bred?"

When I told him, he responded with excitement, "That means he was born three weeks early." He explained that the eyes of premature colts are often not fully developed. Research studies showed that the eyes can still develop within a couple weeks after birth. "Bring him back in two weeks."

In the days that followed, I slipped into the stall frequently and waved my hand in front of Obadiah's long eyelashes, waiting for some kind of response. Four days later, he shifted his head as if he could see shadows. In a few more days, he blinked when my finger neared his eye.

Two weeks later I stood in the clinic while Dr. Roulette shined a flashlight into the colt's eyes. When he was done, a grin slid across his face, "His eyes are normal! He can see just fine."

I jumped up and down and hollered, "Yes!"

Obadiah snorted and hauled back on the lead rope. I laughed. He stood with all four feet braced. As I rubbed him, he melted with relief and leaned into my hand. I looked at the doctor. "Thank you for giving me the encouraging words to wait. It saved this little guy's life."

I am still under the impression there is nothing alive quite so beautiful as a thoroughbred horse.

JOHN GALSWORTHY

*Hope is the last lingering light of the human heart. It shines when every other is put out.*

JAMES H. AUGHEY

"I know the plans I have for you," says the LORD. "They are plans for good and not for disaster, to give you a future and a hope."

THE BOOK OF JEREMIAH NLT

O FOR

Heaven may have happiness as utterly unknown to us as the gift of perfect vision would be to a man born blind.

CHARLES CALEB COLTON

# A HORSE WITH WINGS!

WILLIAM SHAKESPEARE

# *H*idden

The alarm beeped. I reached out of my warm sleeping bag and hit the snooze bar—again. My muscles ached as I rolled over and pulled the brown sleeping bag over my head. *It won't be a big deal if I sleep in a half hour. The boss isn't coming out until later this afternoon.* I'd been hired to gentle 19 wild mules and 1 horse. Only yesterday I'd been kicked, stomped into the mud, and run over. I was exhausted and bruised from head to toe. I reset the alarm and fell fast asleep. The next time the alarm sounded, the sun was streaming in the bunkhouse window.

By the time I splashed water on my face and ate breakfast, the clock showed 8:30, an hour later than usual. *The boss won't notice. Besides I needed the extra rest,* I rationalized. I meandered over to the tack room, pulled a couple halters off some hooks, and hung them over my shoulder. My boots crunched on the gravel as I wandered down the lane to the pasture.

The light from the rising sun glowed off the mountain peaks and a cool breeze skittered a leaf across the lane. Glancing into the tree-studded pasture, I saw the horses and mules on the far side. I stepped over to the fence and put my foot on the bottom strand of barbed-wire and pushed down. The wire squealed as it stretched. I slid through and hiked across the pasture, the morning dew clinging to my boots and jeans.

When I was within 100 feet of the herd I noticed something strange. Belgium, a palomino draft mule stood behind the trunk of a skinny aspen tree. He was facing me, but his head was hidden by the tree. The tree covered his face, but the rest of his body looked like an enormous balloon billowing behind the tree. I glanced sideways. Minnesota, a lanky black mule, had his head behind a tree too. And so did Johnston, a bay mule. They were hiding from me. *They think I can't see them.* I laughed and pretended to sneak through the trees, "Hi, Belgium. I can see you! Silly boy, you can't get out of work that easy."

I sucked in my breath. In that instant I saw myself hiding behind the tree with my body billowing around it. That's what I'd done when I slept in late. My boss might not have found out, but I knew it was wrong. And God had been watching me. *Oh Lord, I'm sorry. It does matter. I'll make up the time by working late.*

Pulling a halter off my shoulder, I eased around the tree. I quickly slipped the lead rope around Belgium's neck, "You can't hide from me." I chuckled, "And *I* can't hide from God."

# Far and away the best prize that life offers is the

*Round-hoofed, short-jointed, fetlocks shag and long,*
*Broad breast, full eye, small head, and nostril wide,*
*High crest, short ears, straight legs and passing strong,*
*Thin mane, thick tail, broad buttock, tender hide:*
*Look what a horse should have he did not lack,*
*Save a proud rider on so proud a back.*

WILLIAM SHAKESPEARE

Blessings we enjoy daily;
and for most of them,
because they be so common,
most men forget to pay
their praises; but let not us,
because it is a sacrifice so
pleasing to Him that made
the sun and us, and still
protects us, and gives us
flowers and showers and
meat and content.

IZAAK WALTON

No hour of life is
wasted that is spent
in the saddle.

WINSTON CHURCHILL

Whenever you are to do a thing,
though it can never be known but to
yourself, ask yourself how you would
act were all the world looking at you,
and act accordingly.

THOMAS JEFFERSON

chance to work hard at work worth doing. THEODORE ROOSEVELT

There on the tips of fresh flowers feedeth he;
How joyous his neigh...there in the midst
of sacred pollen hidden,
all hidden he; how joyous his neigh.

NAVAJO SONG

# Lashing Wind

"Are you ready for a great ride?" I asked Amarillo as I slipped the bit into his mouth and slid the headstall over his ears. This trip was my first time riding the Continental Divide. I'd been amazed at how the wind constantly screamed over the top of the cliffs. Little did I know that before this day was over, the ruthlessness of the high country weather patterns would change my life forever.

The first of the black billowy clouds rolled over the lip of Scapegoat Mountain. At the edge of the meadow, Larry, my boss, sat on his Arabian bay gelding. Studying the sky, he zipped up his brown vest. I stepped into the saddle and rode up to him. "What do you think?"

Larry frowned, "We need to get out of here." He gathered his reins. "I'll lead and have the guys pull string behind me, then you, followed by the guests."

I shouted above the wind to the guests, "Follow me," and I studied the trail. In a hundred yards it narrowed to only a couple-foot wide ledge.

The ominous clouds shot in a stream over the cliff, and then rolled in an arc to the floor of the meadow. Like an enormous Ferris wheel, they circled faster and faster. A blast buffeted us with so much power it pushed Amarillo sideways a few inches.

I shuddered and glanced back at the guests. Their eyes were wide with fear. I squeezed my legs tight and leaned into the wind. I watched in horror as Amarillo's hooves slid an inch closer to the edge. *God, what do I do?* I pleaded. *Help us.*

I was creating too much wind resistance by being on Amarillo. Carefully, I dismounted while clutching the reins. I turned and indicated to the guests that they should dismount too. Suddenly a gust grabbed my batwing chaps and pulled me off my feet. My shoulder slammed the ground. I clawed the trail. My fingers clutched loose stones. Then I saw the boulder. Using all my strength I heaved my body toward the boulder and wrapped my arms around it. *Thank You, God, for this rock.*

My fingernails dug into the indentations. I forced my thoughts toward God. *God, You are my rock. In You I shall trust.* The more I focused on His Word, the bolder my thoughts. *You are my Deliverer. You will get us safely off this mountain. You are Almighty.* I felt something nudging my back. I turned and looked into Amarillo's soft brown eyes. Tears flowed down my cheeks. Corralling my emotions, I forced my thoughts back to God. *You, God, are more powerful than this storm. We will get off this mountain. Help me be strong for the guests.*

Ten feet down the trail was another boulder. Pulling my feet underneath me, I crouched. *God, You hold the winds in Your hand. I'm trusting that You'll tell me when to move.*

Focusing on the next boulder, I waited. Suddenly, in my spirit I heard, "Move!"

Adrenaline rushed through me. Staying low, I shuffled forward, digging one boot into the shale and then the other. Behind me Amarillo carefully picked his way. *Only one more step.* Once again I dug in my boot and then I wrapped my arms around the boulder. I turned and saw that the guests were following my lead.

THE LORD IS MY ROCK, MY FORTRESS, AND MY SAVIOR; MY GOD IS MY ROCK, IN WHOM I FIND PROTECTION.

THE BOOK OF SAMUEL NLT

*They hear a voice in every wind,*
*And snatch a fearful joy.*

THOMAS GRAY

A torrent of wind howled down the rockslide, blasting dust and small stones at me. The next boulder was only about eight feet away. I waited. *God, You are my strong tower. You are my fortress.*

Once again from within my spirit I heard, "Move."

Up the trail I went, capturing one boulder at a time as God urged. Gradually the wind eased. By the time we topped Scapegoat Mountain, the brunt of the storm had passed. I stepped to the side of Amarillo, "Good job, buddy." I turned and encouraged the guests with a wave as they slowly caught up and joined me.

I swung into the saddle as my mind churned. At the beginning of the storm I had pleaded to God for help. But while I clung to the boulder, a new understanding about God flowed through my spirit. All He wanted from me was to have faith in His power, His ability, and His love for me. As I tightened my focus on who He is, He gave me the strength and wisdom to survive.

Sitting around the campfire that night, all of us shared our personal battles on weathering the storm. For me, clinging to the boulders gave me a solid nugget of faith I will carry with me the rest of my life.

There is moreover something magnificent, a kind of majesty in his whole frame, which exalts his rider with pride as he outstrips the wind in his course.

PAULUS JOVIUS

*What delight to back the flying steed that challenges the wind for speed!...Whose soul is in his task, turns labour into sport!*

JAMES SHERIDAN KNOWLES

THEY HAVE IN THEMSELVES WHAT THEY VALUE IN THEIR HORSE, METTLE AND BOTTOM.

RALPH WALDO EMERSON

Have you given the horse its strength or
clothed its neck with a flowing mane?
Did you give it the ability to leap like a locust?
Its majestic snorting is terrifying!
It paws the earth and rejoices in its strength
when it charges out to battle.
It laughs at fear and is unafraid.

THE BOOK OF JOB NLT

48